The Future of the Greek Language and Culture In The United States

Survival In The Diaspora

A REPORT FROM THE ARCHBISHOP'S COMMISSION
ON GREEK LANGUAGE AND HELLENIC CULTURE

John A. Rassias, Commission Chair
Peter Bien, Recorder

James Alatis
John Brademas
Effie Papatzikou Cochran
Michael S. Dukakis
Phyllis Franklin
Ernestine Friedl
Sol Gittleman
Dimitri Gondicas
Mary Ann S. MacLean
David Millstone
John Oller

Vasos Papagapitos
Nicholas Patrikalakis
Peter Patrikis
Paul Sarbanes
Manita Scoccimara
William Scott
Olympia Snowe
Demosthenes P. Sofronas
Anthony Stefanis
Constance Tagopoulos
Jean Van Buskirk

A publication of the
Greek Orthodox Archdiocese of America

Greek Orthodox Archdiocese of America

Office of Print and Digital Media
8-10 East 79th Street, New York, NY 10021
Tel.: (212) 774-0207 Fax: (212) 774-0215
E-mail: digitalmedia@goarch.org

Printed in the United States of America

First printing: June 1999
ISBN 1-58438-014-4
Library of Congress Catalog Card Number: 99-73522

Statement of His Eminence Archbishop Spyridon
On the Report of the Commission on Greek Language and Hellenic Culture

May 27, 1999

I am very happy and proud to present the members of the Commission and their report, "The Future of the Greek Language and Culture in the United States: Survival in the Diaspora" to all of you this morning, for it stands as a landmark achievement in the life of our Holy Archdiocese. When I assumed my responsibilities for the welfare of this Archdiocese from the hands of our Holy Mother Church, I became immediately aware that the issues of Greek language and culture were in dire need of immediate attention.

The eminent Russian Orthodox theologian Father George Florovsky pointed out throughout his long and distinguished career, that Greek language and culture cannot be divorced from Orthodox Christianity. In fact, the loss of the Greek language in Western Europe was a direct cause of the misunderstandings and eventual break between the Western and Eastern Churches. The value of keeping faith and continuity with the language of the New Testament, and for that matter of the Old Testament in the Septuagint, as well as the language of the Church Fathers, cannot be underestimated. If I may quote him:

"The Orthodox Church of East has been speaking for centuries the same old idiom of the Fathers, has kept and cherished it as her true mother tongue, and for that reason is perhaps better equipped for its adequate interpretation than anyone who would merely learn a foreign tongue in order to interpret ancient texts with some respectable dictionary in his hands."

So it is not merely a matter of culture, but also a matter of Faith that the vitality of the Greek language be preserved and cultivated.

Our Church has arrived at a point in its history where the knowledge of the modern Greek language among the majority of our flock is at an all-time low. This cannot reasonably be attributed to the pastoral decision of thirty years ago to employ English in the liturgical services of the Church, because, as is well known, the language of the Liturgy is not spoken Greek. In fact, one could make the argument that the use of English in the Liturgy and the subsequent accessibility of the Liturgy for converts has increased the knowledge of Modern Greek among those very converts who choose to learn Greek as part of their experience of the richness of our Church.

However, the fact remains that the knowledge of Greek is waning in our Archdiocese and with that, the knowledge and appreciation of Hellenic Culture. This does mean to imply that to appreciate Greek Paideia and the Hellenic Ideals one must speak Greek. This is clearly not the case and is demonstrated in the wider society by the Philhellenic spirit of America. But it does mean that in our Greek-American subculture, where the Greek language is allowed to disappear, it is inevitable that the appreciation of Hellenic Culture will also fade.

Is this to say that the primary purpose of the Church is to teach Greek language and culture? By no means. The primary mission of the Church is to preach and teach the Gospel of our Lord Jesus Christ. But we are also the inheritors of a great legacy, and in a country and time when the appreciation of cultural diversity and ethnic origins are a hallmark of our educational systems, what a shame it would be for our own community to lose the very thing that other faith and ethnic communities are striving to maintain.

For all these reasons and more, and I mean the valiant and noble efforts that are made around our beloved Archdiocese every day by hard-working men and women to make the Greek language and culture alive for our children, I asked Professor John A. Rassias of Dartmouth University to head up a commission to study comprehensively the situation as it stands now, and to propose a means by which we can move forward.

I am very pleased to welcome Professor Rassias and members of the Commission to the Archdiocese today, so that they might present the results of their year-long labor of love for the sake of our Church and our children.

CONTENTS

May 27, 1999

Archbishop Spyridon
Primate of the Greek Orthodox Church in America
Greek Orthodox Archdiocese of America
8-10 East 79th Street
New York, NY 10021

Your Eminence:

Your Commission on Greek Language and Hellenic Culture has completed its assignment. Although we witnessed much that is commendable, we also encountered areas of disturbing weakness in the system. Our report therefore includes carefully considered analysis as well as recommendations for action that we present to you with a sense of great urgency.

On March 12, 1998, at our first meeting, you charged us to conduct such public hearings, inquiries, and studies as might be necessary to make recommendations to you. We were charged to consider: (a) the importance of the study of Greek language and culture, (b) the need for professional development, (c) the quality of materials and realia used in instruction, (d) the effectiveness of curricula, (e) the optimal age to begin studying the Greek language and culture, (f) the quality of teacher preparation and retraining, (g) the availability of testing mechanisms, (h) the financing of Hellenic education, (i) the role played by parents, and (j) other areas of importance.

Since March 1998, we have held public hearings in Boston, New York (Manhattan, Flushing), Chicago, Baltimore, and Los Angeles. We have visited Greek schools and have had the opportunity to interview teachers and students. We have also mailed questionnaires in both Greek and English, along with letters in both languages, to Greek teachers and principals of day and afternoon schools in the 500 communities in the United States. To assure greater independence of view, we indicated that the questionnaires need not be signed. We have given many interviews to newspapers and on the radio, have been contacted personally by interested parties, and have issued five interim reports to Commission members.

We gleaned a wide cross section of opinions in extensive personal notes and letters, along with questionnaires from throughout the United States. The questionnaires were evaluated and analyzed by professional statisticians. The results, which may be seen in appendices to this report, underscore many existing problems and substantiate the need for action. The public hearings gave large numbers of people the opportunity to air their feelings.

The makeup of the Commission assured us of the most qualified people to undertake a task of this magnitude. We also had the advantage of a propitious mix of Commissioners born in Greece, members who are Greek-American, and those who are not of Greek heritage. This assembly of people with different backgrounds was essential to arrive at an unbiased consensus on major issues. The expertise of various members was brought to bear in the report, with objectivity being the hallmark. I believe that a Commission made up of a completely Greek constituency would not have had the same degree of impartiality. People some-times view their problems in too narrow a context, whereas the proper context is frequently much broader. Basically, the problems of second-language instruction are not peculiar to the Greek community. Other groups face similar problems, and the Commission considered some of their solutions.

You will find our report to be a well-balanced document that is concerned wholly with what is fitting and proper for the reformation of Greek studies in the Greek Orthodox communities of this nation. We commend you on your initiative, desire for objectivity, and unstinting moral support throughout our investigation.

Measured by the impassioned participation in our hearings and by responses to our questionnaires, I can assure you that the Commission's activities have stimulated, at the very least, an increased interest in improving the instruction of the Greek language and of Hellenic culture. We trust that our report will generate wide public discussion. We believe that the Greek community's school system is ready to receive the Commission's recommendations and, under your leadership, to act on them.

On behalf of the Commission,

Sincerely yours,

John A. Rassias
Chair of the Commission

PREAMBLE

The basic question is how Greek-Americans can thrive as Hellenes in the diaspora. We used to take for granted that students in the Greek schools were Greek and spoke Greek at home. These students now tend to be second, third, or fourth generation, and many come from mixed marriages. They do not speak Greek at home. Or, if one parent does speak Greek to them, they answer in English. Nevertheless, most of the students in Greek school are proud to be Greek. So the schools' task becomes how to preserve and enhance this Hellenic consciousness. How can parents be induced to speak some Greek at home when the children are tired, when they want to watch television or go out to play instead of studying or hearing Greek? How can children overcome their conviction that Greek is useless for them?

One second-generation mother spoke movingly about her own situation. "Why," she asked, "should my third-generation child learn Greek?" There must be a real answer. It can no longer be assumed that learning Greek is the right way to go.

Here is what we learned in our hearings from parents and children when we asked the question, "Why should children learn Greek?"

- Because we are proud to be Greek.

- Because I like the history, people, and culture of Greece.

- Because Greek culture is basic to understanding Western civilization.

- Because I want to communicate with relatives and friends when I go to Greece.

- Because learning another language will help me to become a complete person.

- Because knowledge of another language enhances self-esteem.

- Because knowledge of Greek helps one with English, since so many English words are derived from Greek.

- Because knowledge of a second language generally enhances performance in school in other subjects and leads to higher scores on the SATs.

- Because the New Testament is written in Greek, and I would like my children to be able read it in the original.

- Because I would like to write letters to my friends and relatives in Greece.

- Because knowledge of foreign languages helps a person secure a job in today's global culture.

- Because learning Greek or any other foreign language enables a person to relate to the world in more than one way.

An important question that we heard again and again is whether a heritage can be maintained if its language is lost. Some people argue that if language is forced on children, or taught badly (or both), then the net result is hatred of both the language and the heritage. It might be better to teach the heritage (e.g., ancient Greek mythology, Byzantine civilization, modern Greek culture) via English at first, so that students become interested enough to want to learn the language. Other people maintain that the language must be taught early and in a sustained manner. The Commission agrees. However, the Commission also believes that greater use should be made of English at early stages to teach the Greek heritage.

Achieving competency in the Greek language and acquiring a meaningful awareness of Hellenic culture will require a major, sustained effort. The Commission concludes that these goals cannot be achieved without substantial improvements in the entire system. As the Commission interacted with people throughout the nation, it realized that there are many administrators and teachers who are making laudable contributions to language study. We have reason to rejoice, for the Greek schools do have teachers who are competent, enthusiastic about teaching, and able to respect their students as whole persons - who help their students overcome their fear of learning, fear of making mistakes, who banish boredom and, in sum, make learning an enjoyable experience. To say that problems exist in the system as a whole does not diminish these achievements. However, the Commission has identified persistent structural and systemic problems. These include:

- Inadequate preparation of teachers at all levels.

- A lack of appropriate, pedagogically sound teaching materials.

- A lack of imaginative curricula that touch, excite, and motivate students.

- A lack of uniform standards and criteria for evaluation and testing
  of language proficiency.

- Poor articulation from level to level.

- Insufficient administrative and financial support in many parishes.

- Lack of recognition of good teachers.

- Grossly inadequate compensation and fringe benefits for teachers.

- Inadequate use of technological resources - e.g., computers,
  audio-visual materials, and distance learning.

- Lack of lending libraries with relevant books in Greek and English
  for all ages.

Before we present our findings and recommendations, let us take a moment to dream. How beneficial it would be if Greeks were able to retain their Hellenic ethnicity in the American diaspora while constituting a "Platonic village" in which diversity is strength - i.e., a community in which all people know that they have a task and willingly pursue their own task while at the same time accepting the activities of others as proper within the overall structure. And also, how beneficial it would be if Greeks, like other religious and cultural groups in the United States, could establish excellent schools that serve the population at large. We have every reason to believe that, with effort and determination rooted in the fundamentals of the rich Greek heritage, the Greek community could do this. Indeed, we believe that the Hellenic-American community could create a distinguished institution of higher learning that would stand proudly beside a Catholic Georgetown, a Jewish Brandeis, and a Quaker Haverford!

SUMMARY

The basic questions are how Greek-Americans can thrive as Hellenes in the diaspora and whether their Greek heritage can be maintained if its language is lost. The Commission believes that it cannot. The Greek language is essential; it must be taught early and in a sustained manner. However, English can be used effectively at early stages to teach the Greek heritage to younger students and to instill in them a desire to learn the Greek language.

Although sporadically successful, the present system of language instruction in Greek Orthodox community schools suffers from persistent problems. The Commission's report divides these problems into nine categories:

1. *Morale.* In all three groups that the Commission investigated - teachers, students, and parents (not to mention priests in some cases) - skeptical attitudes exist that undermine the vibrant, joyful instruction of Greek.

2. *Parents.* A disappointingly small percentage of Greek-American parents send their children to Greek school and maintain the Greek language at home.

3. *Organization.* The schools suffer from lack of coordination among themselves and with the public school system.

4. *Curriculum.* There is a paucity of articulated curricula that would enable a better progression from lower to higher grades and allow students to sit for a common examination. There is also a significant underutilization of literature in the curriculum.

5. *Educational materials.* Greek schools need more and better educational materials; their books and ancillary materials do not always match what is available in French, Spanish, Japanese, etc. Materials that may have been

appropriate in the past are now outdated. Children's needs and circumstances have changed. Some of the books now employed fail to relate to American ways and are particularly inappropriate for students from mixed marriages.

6. *Pedagogy.* Greek parochial schools need to match the public schools and other parochial schools in their awareness of diverse and effective methodologies. Especially needed are strategies to de-emphasize grammar and to teach Greek as a foreign language.

7. *Teacher Preparation.* Teachers need training and retraining. Speaking Greek as a mother tongue does not alone qualify one to teach. Teachers from Greece need to become aware of American ways. All teachers need to be trained in how to overcome boredom, how to integrate language with culture, and how to make full use of technological aids, among other strategies.

8. *Compensation.* If schools are to maintain quality education, they must pay their teachers a viable salary along with appropriate benefits. At present, teachers' salaries are grossly inadequate. Of those who responded to our teachers' questionnaire, only 3% indicated satisfaction with their remuneration while 75% indicated that they were not at all satisfied.

9. *Finances.* The burden of financing should rest primarily on the individual parish, not on the Archdiocese or the Greek government. Local fund-raising energizes the individual community and deepens its commitment to language study.

The Commission's report provides seventy-three recommendations, to be implemented on the national or local level, for improvement in the above categories.

The Commission is convinced that, unless action be taken immediately, Hellenism's survival in the American diaspora will be at risk.

CHAPTER I

MORALE: *Successes and Shortcomings*

The Commission found many reasons for optimism. The speakers in our hearings were all sincere in their determination to maintain the Greek heritage. There was frequent applause for the many testimonies about pride in teaching for "the glory of Hellenism."

We were heartened as well by many stories about success in language instruction and about supportive parents who believed in the quality of their schools. We were impressed by the warm, caring environment created by the faculty and administration in some of the schools we visited, by the excellent rapport between students and teachers, by the exceptionally good behavior of the children, and by the intelligent answers given to our questions in most cases.

Good morale is achieved when all elements in a given parish - the priest, the teachers, and the parents - work in harmony. In such cases, the effect on students is predictably positive. For example, when a parish holds an open house, students are given the opportunity to demonstrate what they have learned and to bask in the approval of their parents and other community members. There can be few recruiting devices more effective than seeing excited children demonstrating their learning and their pride in their accomplishment. As one principal reported to the Commission, "These students have a positive ethnic self-image - they know who they are."

On the other hand, the Commission found many reasons for concern. We encountered a pervasive feeling that, historically, the Archdiocese has not always given high enough priority to its educational mission. Furthermore, we were told that some priests do not believe in Greek language education and sometimes do not even speak Greek very well themselves. Whenever the local priest is genuinely interested in Hellenic culture and is competent in the Greek language, he can generate the resources and create the needed programs to promote their instruction. Conversely, priests who cannot effectively use Greek in worship, sermons, and general conversation, and who are adversely predisposed to Hellenic culture, produce the opposite effect: They can divide the community along linguistic lines, with the result that the importance of the Greek language and culture in the parish rapidly declines.

Teachers ardently desire more moral support from the Church and more recognition for their services. In many instances, they feel discouraged by the mix of Greek-speaking and non-Greek-speaking children in the classroom. In all instances, they feel scandalously underpaid. They are equally distressed by the paucity of hours of instruction allowed, by the lack of adequate materials, and by what they perceive as parental indifference.

The Commission, too, is discouraged to hear teachers and priests decry the indifference of the great majority of Greek-American parents, who do not send their children to Greek school and who apparently do not believe in the value of Greek language education. It was even reported in one hearing that converts are often more devoted to Greek than are Greek-Americans.

A further cause for concern is the general lack of self-esteem on the part of Greek-American students unable to compete with Greek-speaking students newly arrived from Greece. In an attempt to assess why student motivation was low, we examined the reactions of high school students to issues related to their education and the Greek language. In one school, the students remained silent, having no answers to any of our questions. We fear that this demonstrates a lack of true motivation in the students themselves, which in turn indicates this school's failure to communicate to its students convincing reasons for the study of Greek.

Taken together, the above problems add up to skepticism, and even to demoralization.

Recommendations:

National

- 1.1 The Archdiocese should consider how best to demonstrate its ongoing commitment to the teaching of the Greek language and Hellenic culture.

- 1.2 Seminarians should be required to take intensive courses in the Greek language during the early part of their studies, and if possible to assist in some parish in Greece during or immediately after their education.

- 1.3 The Archdiocese should establish a central location where those who teach Greek can be prepared and where other relevant training for specific purposes can take place.

- 1.4 In order to enhance students' self-esteem and the credibility of the teaching program, the Archdiocese should award a diploma to children who finish the eighth grade and pass a proficiency examination.

- 1.5 *The Orthodox Observer* should run a page devoted to education as frequently as possible on which it prints examples of writing and/or art work by students from different grades.

- 1.6 At the start of the school year, each school should hold an open house, inviting parents to meet with teachers and some past students in order to learn about the school's program. At this time, past students should demonstrate their competence through recitations, shorts plays, skits, or other means.

- 1.7 Schools should involve parents in recruiting along the lines of "Each-one-reach-one."

- 1.8 Throughout the school year, each school should hold programs in which role models from various professions and vocations speak about how the knowledge of Greek has enriched their lives. Such talks could also be broadcast on Greek radio stations and TV programs.

- 1.9 Use radio announcements and advertisements in local newspapers as ways of bringing the schools to the public's attention.

We teach in order to bring to life, through language,

the gifts God gave us by which to communicate, to share, to help -

in sum, to live fully. We teach in order to activate not only the mind but

also the senses and emotions. Children need to be taught how to look and

really see, how to listen and really hear, how to smell and be pleased or

shocked, how to taste and react, and - most important - how to touch, that

they may be spiritually touched. When all of this is accomplished,

language instruction becomes truly humanistic.

CHAPTER 2

PARENTS: *A Crucial Role*

Language is best mastered at school if the home environment is supportive either through parents who speak Greek or non-Greek-speaking parents who encourage their children's efforts.

Unfortunately, the Commission heard consistent testimony that the schools' problems are caused in large measure by uncooperative or indifferent parents who do nothing at home to encourage their children to speak or understand Greek.

An extremely small percentage of Greek-American children are sent to Greek school. There are several reasons. We were told that in some mixed marriages Greek schooling is opposed out of deference to the non-Greek spouse, if not out of apathy or antagonism. Some parents object to driving considerable distances to deliver their children to school; others say that they cannot afford the tuition, especially when more than one child is involved. Also, in cases where children are sent, all too often the Greek school is used primarily as a baby-sitting facility.

Even when parents are cooperative, they find it difficult to maintain the Greek language at home. Children have so many competing interests: television, sports, clubs, and all sorts of other distractions that youngsters conjure up to avoid studying.

Furthermore, parents all too often permit their children to be absent from class for inadequate reasons. This detracts from the seriousness of the enterprise, discouraging both teachers and assiduous students.

Given such difficulties, one must be thoughtful and considerate when reaching out to parents who do not send their children to Greek school. In cases where the marriage is mixed (a very common situation, indeed true of 80% of the marriages performed in one of the populous parishes we visited), advocates of Hellenic education must be particularly alert not to offend the non-Greek spouse. The wrong approach would be the supernationalistic one. Parents who do not speak Greek need to be sensitized so that they will become partners in the teaching endeavor. They need to recognize the advantages (and also the problems) of bilingualism.

Recommendations:

National

- 2.1 Prepare a handbook for parents on how they can help
  their children at home; include information about resources
  on the Internet.

- 2.2 Design courses in Greek culture for non-Greek-speaking
  parents, taught in English.

Local

- 2.3 Offer effective language courses to non-Greek-speaking
  parents as well as to their children.

- 2.4 Encourage Greek-Orthodox parents to become involved in
  Church affairs in order to acquire a more complete experience
  of Greek culture.

- 2.5 Encourage all parents, especially those of younger children,
  to remain in the classroom whenever possible.

- 2.6 Encourage Greek-speaking parents to serve as teaching aides
  in the classroom.

- 2.7 Reward cooperative parents with reduced tuition
  fees - for instance, those who participate actively in
  the "Each-one-reach-one" program.
  (Judicious means will be needed to do this fairly.)

- 2.8 Vigorously discourage absenteeism.

- 2.9 In each parish, form a cadre of satisfied parents eager to
  contact families that do not send their children to Greek school,
  to serve as a welcoming committee for newcomers to the parish,
  and to contact parents of younger children early on in order
  to help establish a positive attitude.

If parents do not value the study of the Greek language or Hellenic culture, their feelings will be passed along to their children and there will be little reason for the children to embark on a difficult path. Schools cannot operate successfully in a vacuum; without parental support they are guaranteed to fail. The problems are threefold: how to involve children in Greek education in the first place, how to teach them effectively once they are there, and how to celebrate their accomplishments so that the cycle will continue.

CHAPTER 3

ORGANIZATION: *Centralization and Coordination*

Teachers from many different European nations testified at a recent symposium in Crete that problems besetting Greek-language education are more dire in the United States than anywhere else, the alleged cause being a lack in the United States of the centralization enjoyed by Greek schools in other countries.

The Commission was told repeatedly that centralization would help provide a network of support for the schools, since in some areas each Greek school operates independently and often in competition with other parish schools. The Commission heard many calls for team-oriented, non-autocratic coordination through the Archdiocesan Office of Education. At the same time, it heard many reminders that every form of organization must be responsive to local conditions, needs, and resources. A balanced approach would facilitate coordination between the Office of Education, diocesan directors of education, parish communities, and the relevant departments in the Greek Ministry of Culture and Ministry of Education. A centralized office would be able to keep all the schools informed about relevant laws, opportunities, outside funding, etc.

Coordination was a repeated topic in the Commission's hearings. Parishes should not compete but should work together. Churches should "pull down their walls," allowing children from their parish to attend the school of another parish if necessary. The varying level of competence among Greek schools creates a problem for the children's preparation for high school and college. Owing to a laissez-faire attitude, many schools now are proceeding independently. Perhaps the number of schools should be reduced and fewer schools maintained, so that the quality of instruction might improve.

Several teachers felt that their schools have lost great numbers of students because of demographic changes in the makeup of neighborhoods. Greek-American parents have left traditional Greek centers and have moved to the suburbs; this forces them to travel considerable distances to deliver and then pick up their children, since the schools cannot afford vans or buses. The principal of one school located in center-city felt that if his school were transferred to the suburbs its enrollment would triple.

Parishioners felt that coordination is also needed between the Greek parochial schools and public high schools, as well as colleges, to ensure that students receive appropriate credit for their level of proficiency in Greek. For example, the Chicago Board of Education now requires that all high school students complete two years of language study in order to graduate. Students who leave the parochial system after the eighth grade and enter a public high school might be eligible for credit, thus speeding their graduation and providing an incentive to study in the earlier grades. By law, the Chicago Board of Education is required to supply a teacher if twenty or more students wish to study a particular language. And, if an individual public school does not have the twenty students required for an additional teacher to be supplied, the Board of Education can arrange for independent study. It would be useful for the Greek schools to know more about possibilities in the public sector. To this end, they will need to be informed about applicable state and federal legislation.

The Commission was saddened by the evident lack of cooperation among various parishes in close proximity. Along with the lack of coordination regarding curricula and examinations, Greek schools often fail to coordinate their extracurricular activities that enhance Greek identity - for example, music, dance, drama, etc.

Recommendations:

National

- 3.1 Empower the Archdiocesan Office of Education with greater financial resources, additional personnel, and more extensive outreach in matters of curricula, teacher training, materials, and finances, provided that local concerns are also honored.

- 3.2 Evaluate the various types of Greek schools periodically, using independent referees.

- 3.3 Create magnet schools at the high school level as centers of excellence capable of attracting non-Greek as well as Greek students.

Local

- 3.4 Discourage competition among schools within close proximity, since this severely restricts the most profitable use of facilities.

- 3.5 Take advantage of educational opportunities in Greek language and culture available through the local public schools in regions where a substantial number of students are studying Greek.

- 3.6 Coordinate extracurricular activities in communities with many parishes so that each year one of the parishes becomes the locus for activities - such as music, dance, drama, etc. - that lead to a greater sense of Greekness.

- 3.7 Develop after-school Greek clubs.

Through friendly, healthy sharing, schools will bolster

their identity and create an atmosphere of mutual respect.

One way to share is through the spelling bee at the elementary level;

another is through quiz bowls at more advanced levels on topics

such as the Odyssey, the New Testament, mythology, or modern

Greek poetry. Sharing in these extracurricular ways will tighten

the bonds among parishes and allow for greater cooperation

in academic matters.

CHAPTER 4

CURRICULUM: *Professionalism and Focus*

The Commission heard that a strong academic program in language and culture - a full curriculum able to compete with other schools - is a sine qua non of a viable educational program. Parents must feel that they are doing the best for their children; children must be able to compete when they reach high school. The parochial schools need to match the public schools in results. They need to be more professional.

Most Greek schools end at the eighth grade; many graduates continue in Catholic high schools. Clearly, most students stop studying Greek too early. On the bright side, one school in New York, ending in eighth grade, graduated students who averaged 90.1% in the Greek Regents four years later. All these children were second generation, and half of them were from mixed marriages.

Many urged that instruction begin as early as possible - i.e., at the prekindergarten level. The establishment of more preschool, nursery, and kindergarten grades is likely to produce significant returns.

There is a dearth of articulated curricula that would enable a better progression from lower to higher grades, would provide clear guidelines for materials appropriate for each level, and would allow students from all schools to sit for a common examination. The Commission recognizes, of course, that different schools may require customized curricula to some degree. However, the curricula currently in use are not sufficiently standardized.

The Commission witnessed courses that utilized literature not only to inform but also to elicit full participation by students. One such class dealt with Book One of the Iliad. The relevant vocabulary, background information on Homer, the poem's overall action, as well as primary metaphors were all covered. Although the instructor lectured, she also encouraged the students to contribute answers to her apt questions. The students' participation was remarkable and their interest was kept alive to the end of the session. The classroom walls were lined with the students' essays on different literary topics and poems. These papers were impressive for their mastery of language, analytical grasp, and creative approach.

It is important to raise philhellenic as well as Hellenic consciousness in order to show how knowledge of the Greek heritage can be useful in appreciating the art and literature of other countries, particularly that of America. This can be accomplished through content-based instruction - i.e., by teaching Greek mythology, drama, Aesop, Homer, modern history and literature, etc., in English. There is little doubt that Greek heritage taught in English has the ability to entice young students, opening the door to further study, including the study of Greek itself.

The Commission was pleased to see two schools with well-equipped computer rooms, one of which was state of the art, with computers at which children aged six to ten were working under the supervision of the teacher. These children were very involved, happy, and creative. Another school had twenty new computers, five of which were already logged onto the Internet. Plans for a second such room are being considered. We lament the lack of similar equipment in most Greek schools. On the other hand, we are wary about overemphasizing technology. The Internet increases the flow of information and heightens communication among people, bringing the entire world into the classroom. These developments cannot be ignored, but ways must be found to make them meaningful and productive without losing sight of the human factor. Technology will be of little value in educating our children if teachers fail in their indispensable function of inculcating and embodying humanistic values. No matter how awesome technology may be, nothing can match the effect of an underpaid, flawed human being who shares knowledge instead of merely dispensing it, and who connects with his or her students.

Recommendations:

National

- • 4.1 Employ articulated curricula addressing the specialized needs of schools teaching Greek as a foreign language primarily, as opposed to schools whose students are mostly native speakers of Greek.

- • 4.2 Set goals for each grade - what children are expected to know and be able to do after first grade, second grade, etc. - comparable to standards set in other languages.

- • 4.3 Develop common examinations similar to standardized examinations in other languages, based on a nationwide curriculum and perhaps on the guidelines established in *Pistopoiisi eparkeias tis ellinomatheias,* published by the Kentro Ellinikis Glossas (Thessaloniki, 1997).

Local

- • 4.4 Concentrate instruction, especially in the early grades, on speaking and understanding, before other linguistic skills are developed.

- • 4.5 Introduce the accomplishments of Hellenic culture across the ages, in Greece and in the diaspora, taught at first in English and then in Greek. In this way, raise philhellenic as well as Hellenic

consciousness through content-based instruction.
Introduce students to ideals in the arts and sciences inspired
by Hellenic civilization.

- 4.6 Start instruction in language and culture earlier, ideally in
  pre-kindergarten; continue instruction beyond the eighth grade.

- 4.7 Increase the number of hours devoted to Greek per week,
  especially in the higher levels.

- 4.8 Make sensible use of the computer, in particular the Internet,
  which already provides many resources for the study of Greek
  culture, geography, art, and so forth.

The role of drama in the classroom cannot be overemphasized. Play-acting fills a great need in the child's world. It becomes a vehicle through which people live out dreams, becoming anyone they choose and doing anything they want. It is the ideal medium through which students of all ages can divest themselves of their inhibitions by assuming different personae. It is particularly important in the early stages, for it is through drama that students realize that they can express themselves without fear of error, since another is speaking through them.

Drama enables students to unlock their potential for language and to experience what language can accomplish. Their confidence is boosted; the satisfaction of participation leads to further involvement. Everything is alive and active. The student is always center stage.

CHAPTER 5

EDUCATIONAL MATERIALS: *More and Better*

There is a consensus that Greek schools have a great need for more and better educational materials; their books and ancillary materials do not match what is available in French, Spanish, Japanese, etc.

Children's needs have changed; there are fewer immigrants from Greece. Materials that may have been appropriate twenty years ago are now outdated. The problem is that many of the books now employed have very little to do with our own children - they do not relate to American ways and are particularly inappropriate for students from mixed marriages.

The problem does not apply only to children. Adult students tend to drop out in the few Greek language courses that exist for non-Greeks in mixed marriages because the teaching materials and methods are unappealing.

Especially lacking in Greek are history books and books about Greek culture in general. Some now in use come from Greece; although the cultural material they present is rich and may serve as ready resource material, their vocabulary tends to be much too advanced for second-language learners.

However, there are wonderful materials written in English about Greek history, literature, culture, and especially mythology. The Commission visited a remarkable elementary school where such materials are used, primarily in an oral manner. Students from this school, having completed a study of Homer, have signed up in record numbers for a Greek mythology course in the local high school, forcing the teacher of that course to revise it consistent with the students' prior learning.

Recommendations:

National

- 5.1 Develop and utilize materials that fulfill the standards established for each level of Greek instruction: preschool, primary school, middle school, high school.

- 5.2 Develop and utilize materials that fulfill the standards established for each type of Greek instruction (i.e., for non-Greek-speaking children, for Greek-speaking children, for adults).

- 5. Develop and utilize materials that respond to the interests and needs of American children in the Greek diaspora.

- 5.4 Take advantage of materials currently being developed in Greece by the Ministry of Education, the Kentro Ellinikis Glossas, the University of Crete, etc.

- 5.5 In developing new materials, seek the help of independent scholars, Greek studies programs, and professional associations in the United States.

- 5.6 Publish a monthly magazine, distributed nationally, that appeals specifically to Greek-American children. This might include simple Greek comic strips, crossword puzzles, and articles, drawings, and/or poems submitted by the children themselves. Aerostato might serve as a model.

- 5.7 Commission bilingual editions of children's books published in Greece.

- 5.8 Establish a biennial, named award in recognition of the best set of materials developed by local teachers.

- 5.9 Maintain open lines of communication between local schools and the Archdiocesan Office of Education regarding teaching materials.

- 5.10 Establish a web site through which teachers may display effective materials, download them, and exchange ideas.

Local

- 5.11 Encourage individual teachers to develop their own materials, consistent with established criteria for curricula, in a way that enables the local environment to be reflected in texts.

- 5.12 Provide study-leave opportunities and compensation to facilitate the development of materials by individual teachers.

- 5.13 Encourage schools to utilize appropriate materials available in English for the instruction of mythology, literature, and culture to younger children. It is likely that older children will want to continue their study of these subjects in Greek.

To make the class meaningful, the teacher needs to learn to make instruction vibrant. Texts either help or hinder this process. Language books are most often inhabited by unreal, cut-along-the-edges personages who come unglued the minute you try to stand them up. Above all, students want to relate to real people and situations - to the truth. After all, they have been raised on instant truth: television brings natural and man-made disasters directly into the living room. Students have seen the world in living color; inadequate language texts often portray it in black, white, or depressing gray. It is important that students know as much about themselves and what touches them as possible.

They should have the opportunity not only to fill their minds with knowledge but also to express their prejudices, sentiments, and other emotions. They should be at ease with themselves and be encouraged to articulate their innermost thoughts - to read and understand their own book within. In this sense, language study is a route to maturity and completeness. Language, if excellently taught, is a kicking, fleeting, growing, protean power whose dynamism will enhance the students' inherent dynamism and creativity.

Chapter 6.

PEDAGOGY: *Programs to Excite and Challenge*

How and to whom Greek is taught must be reviewed. When immigrants arrived en masse to the United States, the language was an extension of what they had learned in Greece. Greek, then, was taught as the first language for many first-generation children. For the second generation it was often taught in the same way, but the results were not the same. It is true that in some instances it was taught as a second language. The theory was good, but the classroom hours and the pedagogy were inadequate. Now, in most instances, we need to consider Greek a foreign language and teach it accordingly.

Too often in the Greek schools an excessive amount of time is devoted to grammar; that is a mistake. Although the study of grammar is an important part of language pedagogy, it must be placed within a meaningful context. Language can be taught in many ways, but the most efficacious way is through the oral-aural method when that method is properly used by well-prepared, linguistically aware teachers. Interdisciplinary elements from culture, mythology, drama, song, and dance should be tightly woven into the lesson, defining the Greek heritage in the process. Full participation by the children needs to be elicited in every classroom hour. Children need to be instructed in ways that are imaginative, joyful, and challenging.

The unsuccessful classes that we observed were conducted mostly in the form of an old-fashioned lecture, with a few simple questions suggesting obvious answers that only three or four students and the instructor herself kept providing. The successful classes that we observed stressed active participation on the part of students and the sheer joy of learning. The children had their hands constantly raised to answer questions and participated vividly in the discussion. They evidently liked what they were doing.

Separate tracks are needed academically (but not extracurricularly) in order to cope with the diversity of students - namely (a) Greek-speaking children, (b) non-Greek-speaking children. This is imperative for more than academic reasons, since non-Greek-speaking children feel embarrassed, even humiliated, when put in competition with Greek-speaking children.

All relevant studies indicate that class size makes a difference. We were pleased that we heard no complaints about class size. We urge Greek schools to keep classes small.

Recommendations:

National

- • 6.1 Assure that all teachers receive preparation in modern pedagogies that address a variety of educational situations and problems, as well as in strategies to cope with such problems.

- • 6.2 Assure that all teachers receive training in the pedagogy of second-language acquisition.

- • 6.3 Enhance the teaching program by trips to Greece - for example, through the Archdiocesan summer camp (Ionian Village) and travel program.

- • 6.4 Enhance the teaching program through summer camps in the United States where Greek is used exclusively.

- • 6.5 Enhance the teaching program by linking cities having Greek schools to sister cities in Greece or Cyprus. (Among other benefits, this will help to involve parents.)

- • 6.6 Enhance the teaching program by pen-pal communication between American students and students in Greece.

- • 6.7 Enhance the teaching program by exploring the Internet to discover resources.

- • 6.8 Enhance the teaching program by utilizing distance learning to reach remote and/or isolated areas.

Oral communication is the key: *At all costs our students must speak!* Speaking is an integral part of our nature; it is through speaking that we learn a language. Active use is the key to mastering vocabulary; a word atrophies quickly not only when it is not used but also when its fullest meaning has not been incorporated into the student's experience and needs. There is nothing radical in this view - it has been known for centuries. As Saint Augustine pointed out in A.D. 389, "Hearing words does not result in learning; . . . we cannot hope to learn words we do not know unless we have grasped their meaning. This is not achieved by listening to the words, but by getting to know the things signified." Reflecting on strategies of language teaching, the Moravian educator John Amos Comenius wrote in 1648: "All things are taught and learned through examples, precepts, and exercises. . . . The exemplar should always come first, the precept should always follow, and imitation should always be insisted on." Further insistence on hands-on application in learning a language was voiced by Pierre Alexandre Lemare, a French grammarian, in 1819: "When for the first time a child hears the command 'Shut the door!' if he does not see a gesture accompanying the order, if he does not see it carried out immediately, he will not know what it means. . . . But if a voice from somewhere shouts 'Shut the door!' and someone rushes up to close it, . . . he perceives the sense of the expression he has heard."

Chapter 7.

TEACHER PREPARATION: *Renewal and Revitalization*

There is broad consensus that teachers need training and retraining. They need to be prepared in language instruction for different levels, for different age groups, and for students whose first language is not Greek. Teachers need to be trained in immersion techniques and in how to integrate language instruction with culture. They need to learn strategies to overcome boredom. Teachers need to be aware of the implications of multiculturalism. They need to get rid of nationalistic, narrow-minded biases that are outdated and that cannot help young Greek-Americans growing up today.

The Commission was distressed to learn that teachers in Greek schools rarely learn new methods. Although some training sessions exist, they are largely ineffective because they tend to expose the teachers to a lecture, whereas the teachers should be experimenting in techniques - hands-on practice - and participating in the exchange of ideas: showing each other what works and what does not work.

The Greek schools must reject the notion that people who want to teach and whose mother tongue is Greek are automatically capable of teaching well. For example, teachers from Greece do not necessarily know how to teach non-Greek-speaking Greek-Americans. In the future, such teachers need to be carefully screened not just for their professional knowledge but also for their motivation and flexibility. And once they get here, they will certainly need further training if they are to begin to understand the quite different culture in which they will be operating. It would be advantageous for teachers to come from American colleges, where a certain number of students are always being trained in the Greek language and culture. Regarding those from abroad, it was suggested that our schools should play host to young Greek interns - not teachers - so that younger people from Greece might experience our ways, and at the same time help in the classroom and develop lasting friendships.

It would be beneficial to hold teaching programs that bring together all teachers in a given city or district, since this would enhance networking among teachers as well as training them in pedagogy. This can best be accomplished through the creation of an American Association of the Teachers of Greek (AATGR), similar to the American Association of the Teachers of French (AATF), etc., which would hold annual meetings, sponsor colloquia on pedagogical strategies, evaluate materials, sponsor book fairs, and perhaps publish a journal.

Recommendations:

National

- 7.1 Through regional seminars and workshops, all teachers should receive periodic training and retraining in both language instruction and methods of teaching literature and culture.

- 7.2 The Archdiocese should subsidize travel and accommodation for those who attend teacher-training workshops.

- 7.3 Teachers who come from Greece should undergo a training program in the specific characteristics of the American educational environment.

- 7.4 Teachers should be evaluated periodically. This evaluation should be done in a spirit of cooperation and camaraderie by competent internal and external evaluators.

- 7.5 Teachers should be given opportunities and incentives to retrain. If they do not accept and/or do not improve after retraining, they should be dismissed.

- 7.6 Teachers should receive a salary increment based on the number of hours of training they undergo each year.

- 7.7 An American Association of Teachers of Greek (AATGR) should be established.

Local

- 7.8 Schools must give priority to the hiring and preparation of a new generation of teachers.

- 7.9 Together with recruiting experienced teachers from Greece, schools should attract young Greeks to come to the United States as interns for a year, and/or should hire Greek graduate and undergraduate students currently enrolled in American universities to assist in the classroom.

- 7.10 Whenever possible, teachers should be drawn from among graduates of American colleges who possess fluency in Greek.

- 7.11 Diocesan-based placement services should be established in order to facilitate the selection of teachers by school principals.

What Do We Seek in a Good Teacher?

Tens of thousands of students trained throughout the world by the Peace Corps, when asked about the qualities that best define a good teacher, responded: "A good teacher should be competent, skillful, and zealous." A teacher who is competent knows the material well; a teacher who is skillful relies on an effective methodology; a teacher who is zealous shares his or her passion for the subject and teaches it with God's inspiration and help - i.e., with enthusiasm.

CHAPTER 8

COMPENSATION AND BENEFITS: *Time for Serious Reconsideration*

The Commission established that present teachers, looking to the future, do not see where enough new teachers will be found. Teaching is a mission for many, it is true, but that is not sufficient. It is doubtful that people will continue to be attracted, given the meager salaries offered. The crucial factor is the teachers' enthusiasm, but they also need to have adequate financial support, health insurance, retirement benefits, etc.

Teachers' salaries are grossly inadequate. Mean salary seems to be about $25 per hour, but is paid only for class time, not for preparation. To obtain a pension from Greece, teachers must work at least eighteen hours per week and have this as their chief employment - requirements that are rarely met.

Because of the unattractive income and lack of benefits that the profession offers, there is a serious shortage of Greek teachers now. In ten years, very few of those who are currently teaching will be active. Therefore, vigorous recruitment should begin immediately.

In the most successful schools we visited, clearly the school's excellence was derived in large part from the high level of salaries paid, which in turn enabled the school to hire - and retain - well-trained teachers.

In sum, teachers need to be rewarded with adequate salaries and benefits, not to mention moral support and recognition.

Recommendations:

National and local

- 8.1 Since it is likely that the pool of teachers will be drastically depleted in the very near future, it is imperative that steps be taken immediately to improve the condition of current teachers in the areas of salary, benefits, periodic training, and recognition. This will make the schools more attractive to those whom they attempt to recruit in the future. Unless this be done, Greek education will proceed at great peril.

- 8.2 Benefits should include financial support for attending professional meetings in the United States and/or Greece, and other forms of professional development.

- 8.3 Professional development should be rewarded by increases in salary.

Chapter 9

FINANCES: *Serious Support and Awards*

It is abundantly clear to the Commission that a great amount of money will be needed to support the recommendations made by the Commission. There are sharply varying opinions in regard to the proper sources of this money - namely, the proportion of funds that should be solicited from the Archdiocese, individual parishes, businesses, individuals, and/or the Greek government.

There are those who believe that the burden of financing should rest primarily on the individual parish, not on the Archdiocese or the Greek government. Local fund-raising energizes the individual community and deepens its commitment to language study. On the other hand, we must recognize that although many Greek-Americans are quite affluent, others do not send their children to Greek school because they cannot afford to do so, especially when they have more than one child.

A community that takes primary responsibility for its own financial viability will no longer need to fantasize about financial support from the Greek government. There are other ways in which the Greek government might play a role - for example, in sponsoring interns.

Although it is probably not feasible or even advisable for the Archdiocese to assume the full burden of financing every school, the Archdiocese should and could match funds raised by individual parishes. Since a community is a collection of diverse people who share important elements in common - such as heritage, language, religion - it is fitting and proper that there be a synergistic relationship among all parties. For example, since a Greek-owned business benefits from Greek customers, it should give back to the community a commensurate amount in the form of contributions.

Recommendations:

Local

- 9.1 The individual parishes should bear the primary responsibility for funding their schools.

- 9.2 In each parish, a sufficient percentage of total dues from all contributors - not just those parents whose children are in Greek school - should be allocated to education. A percentage sufficient to meet school needs might be suggested by the Archdiocese.

- 9.3 Families with more than one child in Greek school should receive reduced tuition for the second, third, or additional children according to a scale such as: first child full tuition, second child 3/4 tuition, third child 1/2 tuition, subsequent children zero tuition.

- 9.4 Parishes should aggressively seek contributions from local businesses.

National

- 9.5 In recognition of the parishes' efforts to fund their schools, the Archdiocese should respond with a program of proportional matching funds.

CODA

A call for Immediate and Decisive Action

The time is ripe for a concerted, strenuous long-term effort to revitalize Hellenic culture and language in the United States: to constitute the "Platonic village" in which diversity is strength. The Greek language - the indispensable manifestation of Hellenic identity - is rapidly eroding. Unless significant remedial action be taken immediately, Hellenism's survival in the American diaspora will be at risk. The Commission's most dire prediction, based on the evidence it has accumulated, is that Greek identity may well be lost in less than a generation.

Appendices

ΕΡΩΤΗΜΑΤΟΛΟΓΙΟΝ

Για την Ελληνικη Κοινοτικη Παιδεια
στις Ηνωμενες Πολιτειες Αμερικης

THE ARCHBISHOP'S COMMISSION
ON GREEK LANGUAGE AND HELLENIC CULTURE
Greek Orthodox Archdiocese of America
New York, New York

Σεπτέμβριος 1998

I. Προσωπικά Στοιχεία

Παρακαλώ σημειώστε όπου απαιτείται και συμπληρώστε τα κενά:

α) *Είμαι δασκάλα/δάσκαλος των Ελληνικών της _____________ τάξης.*

   _____ Γεννήθηκα στην Ελλάδα.

   _____ Γεννήθηκα στις ΗΠΑ ή κάπου αλλού, αλλά όχι στην Ελλάδα

Η ηλικία μου είναι: *μεταξύ 20 και 40 _____ .*

       μεταξύ 40 και 60 _____ .

       πάνω από 60 _____ .

β)   *Είμαι μαθητής των Ελληνικών της _________ τάξης.*

       Είμαι ________ χρονών.

γ) *Είμαι γονέας μαθητού που μαθαίνει Ελληνικά.*

   _____ Γεννήθηκα στην Ελλάδα.

   _____ Γεννήθηκα στις ΗΠΑ ή κάπου αλλού, αλλά όχι στην Ελλάδα.

   _____ Ο/η σύζυγός μου γεννήθηκε στην Ελλάδα.

   _____ Ο/η σύζυγός μου γεννήθηκε στις ΗΠΑ ή κάπου αλλού, αλλά όχι στην Ελλάδα.

   Τόπος καταγωγής μου και/ή του/της συζύγου μου, εάν δεν είναι η Ελλάδα: ___________________________

II. Αξιολόγηση *(να συμπληρωθεί από τους δασκάλους)*

Σε κάθε ερώτηση σημειώστε με κύκλο την περίπτωση που διαλέγετε σαν απάντηση και, όπου απαιτείται, συμπληρώστε τα κενά:

1. Πώς αξιολογείτε την ποιότητα του διδακτικού υλικού που χρησιμοποιείτε;

    φτωχή   μέτρια   καλή   άριστη

2. Ποια βιβλία χρησιμοποιείτε;

    α) ——————————————————————————

    β) ——————————————————————————

    γ) ——————————————————————————

3. Πώς θα αξιολογούσατε τον αριθμό των εβδομαδιαίων διδακτικών ωρών που έχει ορισθεί για κάθε τάξη;

    ανεπαρκή   επαρκή   περισσότερο από επαρκή

4. Πόσες διδακτικές ώρες, εβδομαδιαίως, έχουν ορισθεί για κάθε τάξη σας; _______

5. Πώς θα αξιολογούσατε το ενδιαφέρον και τη συμμετοχή των μαθητών σας μέσα στην τάξη;

    φτωχή   μέτρια   καλή   άριστη

6. Πώς θα αξιολογούσατε τη βοήθεια που παρέχουν οι γονείς στα παιδιά τους;

    φτωχή   μέτρια   καλή   άριστη

7. Το αναλυτικό πρόγραμμα που ακολουθώ

    μου επεβλήθη   μου υπεδείχθη   σχεδιάστηκε εντελώς από μένα

8. Πόσο χρόνο ξοδεύετε για να προετοιμαστείτε για κάθε τάξη;

    Περίπου _______ ώρα(ες).

9. *Πόσο ικανοποιημένη/ος είστε με τις συνθήκες εργασίας σας;*

     καθόλου   αρκετά ικανοποιημένη/ος   πολύ ικανοποιημένη/ος

10. *Διδάσκω εθελοντικώς και δεν λαμβάνω καμμία αμοιβή.*

     _____ Ναι   _____ Όχι

11. *Εάν είστε μισθωτή/ός, πόσο ικανοποιημένη/ος είστε με το μισθό σας;*

     καθόλου   αρκετά ικανοποιημένη/ος   πολύ ικανοποιημένη/ος

12. *Πόσο ικανοποιημένη/ος είστε με τα ευεργετήματα που σας παρέχουν;*
(ιατροφαρμακευτική περίθαλψη, άδειες, κλπ.)

     καθόλου   αρκετά ικανοποιημένη/ος   πολύ ικανοποιημένη/ος

13. *Πόσο συχνά έχετε τη δυνατότητα να πηγαίνετε στην Ελλάδα;*

     σπανίως   αρκετά συχνά   συχνά

14. *Πόσο συχνά διοργανώνονται επιμορφωτικά σεμινάρια από το σχολείο σας;*

     σπανίως   αρκετά συχνά   συχνά

15. *(Εάν γίνονται) Η ποιότητα των επιμορφωτικών σεμιναρίων είναι:*

     φτωχή   καλή   άριστη

16. *Θα θέλατε να έχετε περισσότερα επιμορφωτικά σεμινάρια;*

     _____ Ναι   _____ Όχι

17. *Έχετε αποτελεσματική συνεργασία με κάποιον φορέα;*

     _____ Ναι   _____ Όχι

     (Αν ναι, με ποιον):

     γονείς   PTA   Αρχιεπισκοπή   άλλο

18. *Ποια, κατά τη γνώμη σας, είναι η κατάλληλη ηλικία για να αρχίσει ένα παιδί μαθήματα Ελληνικών;*

_________ χρονών

19. *Αξιολογείστε τις γλωσσικές δεξιότητες στις οποίες πρέπει να δοθεί ιδιαίτερη έμφαση για την εκμάθηση της Ελληνικής γλώσσας, κατά σειρά σπουδαιότητας. Χρησιμοποιείστε την ακόλουθη κλίμακα: 1 = σπουδαιότερη, 2 = 2η σε σπουδαιότητα, 3 = 3η σε σπουδαιότητα, 4 = τελευταία σε σπουδαιότητα*

______ ανάγνωση   ______ γραφή

______ ομιλία   ______ ακουστική αντίληψη

20. *Ποιες θα πρέπει να είναι, κατά τη δική σας άποψη, οι σπουδαιότερες ενότητες στο αναλυτικό πρόγραμμα του σχολείου σας; Χρησιμοποιείστε την ακόλουθη κλίμακα: 1 = σπουδαιότερη, 2 = 2η σε σπουδαιότητα, 3 = 3η σε σπουδαιότητα 4 = 4η σε σπουδαιότητα, 5 = τελευταία σε σπουδαιότητα*

______ πολιτισμός   ______ ιστορία   ______ θρησκευτικά

______ λογοτεχνία   ______ γλώσσα

21. *Αξιολογείστε την αποτελεσματικότητα των οπτικοακουστικών μέσων διδασκαλίας που χρησιμοποιείτε:*

ανεπαρκής   επαρκής   τέλεια

22. *Με ποιον(ους) τρόπο(ους) εξετάζετε τους μαθητές σας; (Βάλτε σε κύκλο ό,τι σας ταιριάζει)*

προφορικές εξετάσεις   γραπτές εξετάσεις

(εάν οι εξετάσεις είναι γραπτές):

εκθέσεις   ερωτήσεις επιλογής   μεταφράσεις

23. *Πόση σχολική εργασία για το σπίτι δίνετε στους μαθητές σας;*

καθόλου   λίγη   αρκετή   πολλή

III. Αξιολόγηση *(Να συμπληρωθεί από τους μαθητές)*

Σε κάθε ερώτηση σημειώστε με κύκλο την περίπτωση που διαλέγετε σαν απάντηση και, όπου απαιτείται, συμπληρώστε τα κενά:

1. Πώς θα αξιολογούσατε την εκπαίδευση που λαμβάνετε στο σχολείο σας;

  φτωχή   μέτρια   καλή   άριστη

2. Πώς θα αξιολογούσατε την ποιότητα του διδακτικού υλικού που χρησιμοποιείτε;

  φτωχή   μέτρια   καλή   άριστη

3. Ποια βιβλία χρησιμοποιείτε;

  α) ____

  β) ____

  γ) ____

4. Πώς θα αξιολογούσατε τον αριθμό των εβδομαδιαίων διδακτικών ωρών που έχουν καθορισθεί για το μάθημα των Ελληνικών από τη διεύθυνση του σχολείου σας;

  ανεπαρκή   επαρκή   περισσότερο από επαρκή

5. Πόσες διδακτικές ώρες την εβδομάδα διδάσκεστε Ελληνικά; __________

6. Τι σας αρέσει καλύτερα;

  προφορική εργασία γραπτή εργασία ανάγνωση γραμματική

7. Τι σας αρέσει λιγότερο;

  προφορική εργασία γραπτή εργασία ανάγνωση γραμματική

8. *Αξιολογείστε τις γλωσσικές δεξιότητες στις οποίες νομίζετε ότι πρέπει να δοθεί έμφαση για την εκμάθηση της Ελληνικής γλώσσας, κατά σειρά σπουδαιότητας. Χρησιμοποιείστε την ακόλουθη κλίμακα: 1 = σπουδαιότερη, 2 = 2η σε σπουδαιότητα, 3 = 3η σε σπουδαιότητα, 4 = τελευταία σε σπουδαιότητα*

    ______ ανάγνωση   ______ γραφή

    ______ ομιλία   ______ ακουστική αντίληψη

9. *Ποιες είναι οι πιο σημαντικές ενότητες στο αναλυτικό πρόγραμμα του σχολείου σας; Χρησιμοποιείστε την ακόλουθη κλίμακα: 1 = σπουδαιότερη, 2 = 2η σε σπουδαιότητα, 3 = 3η σε σπουδαιότητα, 4 = 4η σε σπουδαιότητα, 5 = τελευταία σε σπουδαιότητα*

    ______ πολιτισμός   ______ ιστορία   ______ θρησκευτικά

    ______ λογοτεχνία   ______ γλώσσα

10. *Πόση σχολική εργασία σας δίνεται για το σπίτι;*

    καθόλου   πολύ λίγη   αρκετή   πολλή   πάρα πολύ

11. *(για μαθητές που πρόσφατα ήταν στην Ελλάδα): Όταν ήμουνα στην Ελλάδα αντιλήφθηκα ότι*

    καταλάβαινα πολύ λίγα Ελληνικά

    καταλάβαινα αρκετά Ελληνικά

    καταλάβαινα πολύ καλά Ελληνικά

    μπορούσα να διαβάζω επιγραφές δρόμων

    μπορούσα να διαβάζω διαφημίσεις

    μπορούσα να διαβάζω εφημερίδες

    δεν με καταλάβαιναν

    με καταλάβαιναν λίγο

    με καταλάβαιναν χωρίς δυσκολία

IV. Αξιολόγηση *(να συμπληρωθεί από τους γονείς)*

Σε κάθε ερώτηση σημειώστε με κύκλο την περίπτωση που διαλέγετε σαν απάντηση και, όπου απαιτείται, συμπληρώστε τα κενά:

1. Πώς θα αξιολογούσατε τον αριθμό των εβδομαδιαίων διδακτικών ωρών που το σχολείο του παιδιού σας έχει καθορίσει για το μάθημα των Ελληνικών;

      ανεπαρκή   επαρκή   περισσότερο από επαρκή

2. Πόσες διδακτικές ώρες εβδομαδιαίως διδάσκεται το παιδί σας Ελληνικά; _____________

3. Αξιολογείστε τις γλωσσικές δεξιότητες στις οποίες πρέπει να δοθεί ιδιαίτερη έμφαση για την εκμάθηση της Ελληνικής γλώσσας, κατά σειρά σπουδαιότητας. Χρησιμοποιείστε την ακόλουθη κλίμακα: 1 = σπουδαιότερη, 2 = 2η σε σπουδαιότητα, 3 = 3η σε σπουδαιότητα, 4 = τελευταία σε σπουδαιότητα

    ______ ανάγνωση   ______ γραφή

    ______ ομιλία   ______ ακουστική αντίληψη

4. Κατά τη γνώμη σας, ποιες θα πρέπει να είναι οι πιο σπουδαίες ενότητες στο αναλυτικό πρόγραμμα που χρησιμοποιούν στο σχολείο του παιδιού σας; Χρησιμοποιείστε την ακόλουθη κλίμακα: 1 = σπουδαιότερη, 2 = 2η σε σπουδαιότητα 3 = 3η σε σπουδαιότητα, 4 = 4η σε σπουδαιότητα, 5 = τελευταία σε σπουδαιότητα

    ______ πολιτισμός   ______ ιστορία   ______ θρησκευτικά

    ______ λογοτεχνία   ______ γλώσσα

5. Κατά τη γνώμη σας, πόση σχολική εργασία για το σπίτι πρέπει να δίνεται στο παιδί σας;

      πολύ λίγη   αρκετή   πολλή   πάρα πολύ

6. Μιλάτε Ελληνικά στο σπίτι σας;

      καθόλου   λίγο   αρκετά   πολύ

7. Πόσο συχνά ταξιδεύετε στην Ελλάδα με την οικογένειά σας;

      ποτέ   κάπου-κάπου   συχνά

8. Όταν ταξιδεύετε στην Ελλάδα, πόσο καλά το παιδί σας επικοινωνεί με τους ντόπιους συνομιλητές του;

    πολύ λίγο   αρκετά καλά   πολύ καλά

9. Πόσο αναμεμειγμένη/ος είστε εσείς και η οικογένειά σας με κάποια ελληνική κοινότητα στην Αμερική;

    καθόλου   ελάχιστα   πολύ

10. Είστε συνδρομήτρια/ής σε ελληνόφωνη εφημερίδα ή περιοδικό;

    όχι   ναι

11. Εάν υπάρχει ελληνικό ραδιοφωνικό ή τηλεοπτικό πρόγραμμα στην παροικία σας, πόσο συχνά το ακούτε;

    ποτέ   όχι συχνά   συχνά

12. Το παιδί σας διαβάζει ελληνικά βιβλία στο σπίτι;

    όχι   ναι

13. Μένουν μαζί σας ή κοντά στο σπίτι σας παππούς και γιαγιά που μιλούν Ελληνικά;

    όχι   ναι

14. Κατά τη γνώμη σας, ποιοι είναι οι πιο σπουδαίοι παράγοντες που θα οδηγήσουν το παιδί σας στην επιτυχή εκμάθηση της Ελληνικής γλώσσας και του πολιτισμού μας; Χρησιμοποιείστε την ακόλουθη κλίμακα: 1 = σπουδαιότερος, 2 = 2ος σε σπουδαιότητα, 3 = 3ος σε σπουδαιότητα, 4 = τελευταίος σε σπουδαιότητα

_______ άριστη εκπαίδευση

_______ βοήθεια από το οικογενειακό περιβάλλον

_______ ταξίδια στην Ελλάδα

_______ διαμονή κοντά σε ελληνική παροικία

_______ άλλο (εξηγείστε) ____

15. Το παιδί σας αλληλογραφεί με κάποιο άλλο ελληνόπουλο;

    όχι   ναι

Υποδείξεις για βελτίωση της Ελληνικής Παιδείας

*(Αυτός ο χώρος ανήκει σε όλους: δασκάλους, μαθητές και γονείς.
Σας παρακαλούμε να είστε ειλικρινείς στις παρατηρήσεις σας.
Αν χρειαστεί, χρησιμοποιείστε κι άλλη σελίδα).*

*Σας ευχαριστούμε για το χρόνο σας, το ενδιαφέρον σας
και τη συνεργασία σας.*

Σας παρακαλούμε επιστρέψτε αυτό το Ερωτηματολόγιο στον:

*Professor John A. Rassias
Chair, Archbishop's Commission
6071 Wentworth Hall
Dartmouth College
Hanover, NH 03755*

QUESTIONNAIRE

FOR THE STUDIES OF GREEK LANGUAGE AND CULTURE IN OUR COMMUNITY SCHOOL SYSTEM IN THE USA

THE ARCHBISHOP'S COMMISSION ON GREEK LANGUAGE AND HELLENIC CULTURE

Greek Orthodox Archdiocese
New York, NY

September 1998

I. Personal Background

Please check where appropriate and fill in blanks:

1) I am a teacher of Greek, at the ________________level.

      ____ I was born in Greece.

      ____ I was born in the United States or elsewhere but not in Greece.

My age is: *between 20 & 40 ____;*

                  between 40 & 60 ____;

                          60 ____.

2)   *I am a student of Greek, at the _________ level.*

      I am _________ years old.

3) I am a parent of a student studying Greek.

      _____ I was born in Greece.

      *_____ I was born in the United States or elsewhere,
but not in Greece.*

      _____ My spouse was born in Greece.

      *_____ My spouse was born in the United States or elsewhere,
but not in Greece.*

      Ethnic background of myself and/or my spouse, if not Greek:

      ____

II. Evaluation *(to be completed by teachers)*

Circle one of the choices for each question and, where appropriate, fill in blanks:

1. *How would you rate the quality of the instructional materials used?*

    poor   fair   good   excellent

2. *Which textbook(s) do you use?*

____

3. *How would you rate the number of classroom hours per week?*

    inadequate   adequate   more than adequate

4. *How many classroom hours per week are devoted to each of your classes?* _______

5. *How would you rate the interest and involvement of your students?*

    poor   fair   good   excellent

6. *How would you rate the parents' support of their children?*

    poor   fair   good   excellent

7. *My curriculum is*

    imposed   suggested   designed entirely by me

8. *How much time do you spend preparing for each class? about_______ hours.*

9. *How satisfied are you with your working conditions?*

    not at all   fairly satisfied   very satisfied

10. *I volunteer my teaching and receive no compensation.*

_______ Yes   _______ No

11. *If you receive a salary, how satisfied are you with it?*

not at all   fairly satisfied   very satisfied

12. *How satisfied are you with your benefits? (health insurance, vacations, etc.)*

not at all   fairly satisfied   very satisfied

13. *How often are you able to go to Greece?*

rarely   fairly often   frequently

14. *How often do you have in-house teacher training?*

rarely   fairly often   frequently

15. *(if applicable) The quality of my in-house teacher training is:*

poor   adequate   excellent

16. *Would you like to have additional in-house teacher training?*

_______ Yes   _______ No

17. *Do you have an effective support network?*

_______ Yes   _______ No

If yes: parents   PTA   Archdiocese   other

18. *What in your opinion is the optimal age for beginning the study of Greek?*

_______ *years old*

19. *Rate the skills that you think should be emphasized in language learning, in order of importance. Use the following scale: 1 = most important, 2 = 2nd in importance, 3 = 3rd in importance, 4 = least important*

    ______ reading   ______ writing

    ______ speaking   ______ comprehension

20. *In your opinion, what should be the most important areas in your school curriculum? Use the following scale: 1 = most important. 2 = 2nd in importance, 3 = 3rd in importance, 4 = 4th in importance, 5 = least important*

    ______ culture   ______ history   ______ religion

    ______ literature   ______ language

21. *Rate your supply of effective audio-visual materials.*

    inadequate   adequate   superior

22. *In which, way(s) do you test your students (circle all that apply)?*

        oral exams   written exams

    (if written): essays   multiple choice   translations

23. *How much homework do you give?*

    none   little   a fair amount   much

III. Evaluation *(to be completed by students)*

Circle one of the choices for each question and, where appropriate, fill in blanks:

1. *How would you rate the quality of your instruction?*

       poor   fair   good   excellent

2. *How would you rate the quality of the instructional materials used?*

       poor   fair   good   excellent

3. *Which textbook(s) do you use?*

    ____

4. *How would you rate the number of classroom hours per week?*

      inadequate   adequate   more than adequate

5. *How many classroom hours per week are devoted to Greek in your case?* _______

6. *What do you like best?*

       oral work   written work   reading   grammar

7. *What do you like least?*

       oral work   written work   reading   grammar

8. *Rate the skills that you think should be emphasized in language instruction,
   in order of importance. Use the following scale: = 1= most important, 2 = 2nd in
   importance, 3 = 3rd in importance, 4 = least important*

    _______ reading   _______ writing

    _______ speaking   _______ comprehension

9. *Which have been the most important areas in your school curriculum?*
   Use the following scale: 1 = most important, 2 = 2nd in importance,
   3 = 3rd in importance, 4 = least important

   _______ culture   _______ history   _______ religion

   _______ literature   _______ language

10. *How much homework is assigned?*

    none   too little   fair amount   much   too much

11. *(for students who have been to Greece recently):*
    When in Greece, I found that I could

    understand very little   understand enough

    understand a lot   read street signs

    read advertisements   read newspapers

    not be understood   be poorly understood

    be easily understood

IV. Evaluation *(to be completed by parents)*

Circle one of the choices for each question and, where appropriate, fill in blanks:

1. *How would you rate the number of classroom hours per week?*

    inadequate   adequate   more than adequate

2. *How many classroom hours per week are devoted to your child's instruction in Greek?*_______

3. *Rate the skills that you think should be emphasized in language instruction, in order of importance. Use the following scale: 1 = most important, 2 = 2nd in importance, 3 = 3rd in importance, 4 = least important*

    _______ reading   _______ writing

    _______ speaking   _______ comprehension

4. *In your opinion- what should be the Most important areas in your child's school curriculum? Use the following scale: 1 = most important, 2 = 2nd in importance, 3 = 3rd in importance, 4 = least important*

    _______ culture   _______ history   _______ religion

    _______ literature   _______ language

5. *In your opinion, how much homework is assigned?*

    too little   fair amount   much   too much

6. *How much Greek is spoken in your home?*

    none   a little   a fair amount   a lot

7. *How often do you travel to Greece with your family?*

    never   occasionally   frequently

8. *If you do travel to Greece, how well does your child communicate with native speakers?*

> poorly   fairly well   quite well

9. *How involved are you and your family with a Greek community in America?*

> not at all   minimally   quite a lot

10. *Do you subscribe to a Greek-language newspaper or magazine?*

> yes   no

11. *If there is a radio or TV program in the Greek language in your community, how often do you listen to it?*

> never   infrequently   frequently

12. *Does your child read Greek-language books at home?*

> yes   no

13. *Are there Greek-speaking grandparents living in your household or nearby?*

> yes   no

14. *In Your opinion, what are the most important factors governing your child's successful acquisition of Greek language and culture? Use the following scale: 1 = most important, 2 = 2nd in importance, 3 = 3rd in importance, 4 = least important*

> _______ excellent schooling
>
> _______ a supportive home environment
>
> _______ travel to Greece _______ living in a Greek neighborhood
>
> _______ other (please explain): _________________________________

15. *Does your child have a Greek pen-pal?*

> yes   no

Recommendations for Improvement

*(This section is meant for everyone: teachers, students, and parents.
Please be frank. Use an additional page if necessary.)*

*Thank you for your
time, interest and cooperation.*

Please return this document to:

*Professor John A. Rassias
Chair, Archbishop's Commission
6071 Wentworth Hall
Dartmouth College
Hanover, NH 03755*

APPENDIX C

Subjective Appraisal of the Statistical Data

The statistics in the three questionnaires most often corroborate what the Commission heard at its public hearings; however, divergences do exist.

The Commission finds the following to be most pertinent (percentages have been rounded down):

- 85% of the teachers who responded are in elementary or middle school, whereas only 2% of the respondents are in high school. Of the students who responded, 84% are in elementary or middle school, only 7% in high school.

- 74% of the teachers who responded were born in Greece. Of the parents who responded, 43% were born in Greece and 55% of their spouses were also born in Greece.

- 67% of the teachers who responded are over 40 years old.

- Teachers rated the quality of the materials as follows: poor to fair, 44%; good, 46%; excellent, 8%. Pupils rated the materials more favorably: 22% poor to fair, 52% good, and 26% excellent.

- A majority in all three groups rated classroom hours as adequate: teachers 52%, students 65%, parents 66%. The Commission disagrees.

- Involvement of students was rated as good or excellent by 69% of the teachers.

- Parental support was rated as good or excellent by 41% of the teachers.

- 58% of teachers had to design their own curriculum.

- 76% of teachers spend from 1 to 2 hours preparing for class.

- Both parents and students testified that the average number of hours devoted to Greek per week is 4.

- 78% of the teachers who responded are either not at all satisfied or fairly satisfied with their working conditions. Only 20% are very satisfied.

- 15% of the teachers volunteer services and receive no compensation. Of the 85% who receive compensation, only 9% are very satisfied.

• Only 3% of the teachers are very satisfied with the benefits they receive.

• Only 9% of the teachers indicated that they have frequent in-house training. 71% noted that they rarely had in-house training.

• The quality of in-house training was rated poor by 29% of the respondents, adequate by 62%, and excellent by only 9%.

• 64% of the teachers indicated a need for additional in-house training.

• To the question, "Which skills should be emphasized in language instruction?" teachers answered as follows: speaking, 53%; comprehension, 43%; reading, 18%; writing 7%. Students answered: speaking, 65%; reading, 26%; comprehension 24%; writing, 15%. Parents answered: speaking, 67%; comprehension, 36%; reading, 23%; writing, 14%. Clearly, speaking is considered the most important skill. This corroborates what the Commission heard in its oral testimony.

• To the question, "What do you like best in class?" 42% of the students favored oral work while only 6% favored grammar.

• Regarding what is most important in the curriculum, the percentage of teachers favoring language was 90, the percentage of students 59, the percentage of parents 83. Of the categories language, religion, history, and literature, all groups deemed literature by far the least important. This is in distinct variance with the Commission's view that appropriate literature, well taught, enlivens students and informs them.

• 72% of the teachers rated their support network superior -
an approbation that the Commission did not find in its hearings.

The Commission was pleased to find that the questionnaires corroborate, for most the part, the oral testimony heard throughout the nation as well as the Commission's own conclusions. In addition, we were particularly pleased to have received much extensive, thoughtful, eloquent, and well-written commentary in both Greek and English appended to the questionnaires and offering recommendations, many of which have been included in this Report.

APPENDIX D

Questionnaire for the Studies of Greek Language and Culture
in Our Community School System in the USA   *(N=132)*

I. Personal Background

a) I am a teacher of Greek at the level:

64.7%	Elementary School
19.6%	Middle School
2.0%	High School
13.7%	All levels

I was born:

73.5%	In Greece
20.5%	In the US or elsewhere, not Greece

My age is:

32.8%	Between 20 & 40 years old
50.4%	Between 40 & 60 years old
16.8%	Over 60 years old

II. Evaluation

1. How would you rate the quality of materials used?

8.5%	Poor
35.6%	Fair
48.3%	Good
7.6%	Excellent

2. *Which textbooks do you use?*

    (Titles on file)

____

____

____

____

3. *How would you rate the number of classroom hours per week?*

46.8%	Inadequate
52.4%	Adequate
0.8%	More than adequate

4. *How many classroom hours per week are devoted to each of your classes?*

5.1%	1 hour
28.2%	2 hours
17.9%	3 hours
23.9%	4 hours
9.4%	5 hours
15.4%	6 hours
0.0%	More than 6 hours
3.504	Mean classroom time spent on Greek

5. *How would you rate the interest and involvement of your students?*

8.0%	Poor
23.9%	Fair
56.6%	Good
11.5%	Excellent

6. *How would you rate the parents' support of their children?*

23.2%	Poor
35.7%	Fair
31.3%	Good
9.8%	Excellent

7. *My curriculum is:*

8.7%	Imposed
33.7%	Suggested
57.6%	Designed entirely by me

8. *How much time do you spend preparing for each class?*

25.7%	1 hour
49.6%	2 hours
9.7%	3 hours
8.0%	4 hours
4.4%	5 hours
2.7%	More than 5 hours

9. *How satisfied are you with your working conditions?*

15.9%	Not at all
61.9%	Fairly satisfied
20.3%	Very satisfied

10. *I volunteer my services and receive no compensation:*

15.0%	Yes
85.0%	No

11. *If you receive a salary, how satisfied are you with it?*

43.4%	Not at all
47.2%	Fairly satisfied
9.4%	Very satisfied

12. *How satisfied are you with your benefits? (health insurance, vacations, etc.)*

75.0%	Not at all
21.6%	Fairly satisfied
3.4%	Very satisfied

13. *How often are you able to go to Greece?*

25.8%	Rarely
33.3%	Fairly often
40.8%	Frequently

14. *How often do you have in-house teacher training?*

70.5%	Rarely
21.0%	Fairly often
8.6%	Frequently

15. *(If applicable) The quality of in-house training is:*

28.8%	Poor
62.1%	Adequate
9.1%	Excellent

16. *Would you like to have additional in-house training?*

64.2%	Yes
35.8%	No

17. *Do you have an effective support network?*

71.8%	Yes
28.2%	No

If yes, indicate which of the following are effective:

50.0%	Parents
59.7%	PTA
17.7%	Archdiocese
4.8%	Other

18. *What, in your opinion, is the optimal age for beginning the study of Greek?*

19.5%	Under 5 years old
17.1%	5 years old
25.2%	6 years old
32.5%	7 years old
5.7%	Over 7 years old

19. *Rate the skills that you think should be emphasized, in order of importance.*

    19a. Importance of reading:

18.3%	Most important
24.2%	2nd in importance
55.8%	3rd in importance
1.7%	Least important

    19b. Importance of writing:

6.7%	Most important
13.3%	2nd in importance
15.8%	3rd in importance
64.2%	Least important

19c. Importance of speaking:

52.5%	Most important
35.0%	2nd in importance
8.3%	3rd in importance
4.2%	Least important

19d. Importance of comprehension:

43.2%	Most important
33.9%	2nd in importance
8.5%	3rd in importance
14.4%	Least important

Percentage of people responding "most important"

52.5%	Speaking
43.2%	Comprehension
18.3%	Reading
6.7%	Writing

20. In your opinion, what would be the most important areas in your school curriculum?

20a. Importance of culture:

10.0%	Most important
31.7%	2nd in importance
21.7%	3rd in importance
29.2%	4th in importance
7.5%	Least important

20b. Importance of history:

6.6%	Most important
33.9%	2nd in importance
39.7%	3rd in importance
16.5%	4th in importance
3.3%	Least important

20c. Importance of religion:

13.9%	Most important
28.7%	2nd in importance
23.0%	3rd in importance
17.2%	4th in importance
17.2%	Least important

20d. Importance of literature:

3.5%	Most important
14.8%	2nd in importance
9.6%	3rd in importance
20.0%	4th in importance
52.2%	Least important

20e. Importance of language:

89.5%	Most important
9.7%	2nd in importance
0.0%	3rd in importance
0.8%	4th in importance
0.0%	Least important

Percentage of people responding "most important"

89.5%	Language
13.9%	Religion
10.0%	Culture
6.6%	History
3.5%	Literature

21. Rate your supply of effective audio visual materials.

53.6%	Inadequate
41.8%	Adequate
4.5%	Superior

22. In which ways do you test your students?

83.6%	Oral
90.2%	Written

Of those who give written tests, what percentage give:

52.0%	Essays
65.0%	Multiple Choice
48.0%	Translations

23. How much homework do you give?

0.8%	None
26.4%	Little
66.1%	A fair amount
6.6%	Much

APPENDIX E

Questionnaire for the Studies of Greek Language and Culture
in Our Community School System in the USA *(N=240)*

I. Personal Background

b) I am a student of Greek at level:

45.6%	Elementary
38.2%	Middle school
7.4%	High school
8.8%	All

Age:

10.2%	Under 7 years old
6.5%	8 years old
4.6%	9 years old
14.8%	10 years old
28.7%	11 years old
9.3%	12 years old
15.7%	13 years old
10.2%	Over 14 years old

II. Evaluation

1. How would you rate the quality of your instruction?

2.5%	Poor
12.6%	Fair
55.0%	Good
29.8%	Excellent

2. How would you rate the quality of the instructional materials used?

6.3%	Poor
16.0%	Fair
52.1%	Good
25.6%	Excellent

3. Which textbook(s) do you use?

____

4. How would you rate the number of classroom hours per week?

11.7%	Inadequate
64.9%	Adequate
23.4%	More than adequate

5. How many classroom hours per week are devoted to Greek in your case?

8.1%	1 hour
19.3%	2 hours
19.3%	3 hours
20.6%	4 hours
6.3%	5 hours
11.2%	6 hours
15.2%	More than 6 hours
3.92	Mean classroom time spent on Greek

6. What do you like best?

42.2%	Oral work
18.8%	Written work
33.2%	Reading
5.8%	Grammar

7. *What do you like least?*

17.2%   Oral work

40.3%   Written work

11.8%   Reading

30.8%   Grammar

8. *Rate the skills that you think should be emphasized in language instruction, in order of importance.*

   8a. *Importance of reading:*

25.9%   Most important

29.9%   2nd in importance

32.1%   3rd in importance

12.1%   Least important

   8b. *Importance of writing:*

15.2%   Most important

22.0%   2nd in importance

27.8%   3rd in importance

35.0%   Least important

   8c. *Importance of speaking:*

64.8%   Most important

18.1%   2nd in importance

8.8%   3rd in importance

8.4%   Least important

8d. Importance of comprehension:

23.6%	Most important
26.2%	2nd in importance
17.3%	3rd in importance
32.9%	Least important

Percentage of people responding "most important"

64.8%	Speaking
25.9%	Reading
23.6%	Comprehension
15.2%	Writing

9. Which have been the most important areas in your school curriculum?

9a. Importance of culture:

15.0%	Most important
29.4%	2nd in importance
18.2%	3rd in importance
21.5%	4th in importance
15.9%	Least important

9b. Importance of history:

17.3%	Most important
24.5%	2nd in importance
27.7%	3rd in importance
20.0%	4th in importance
10.5%	Least important

9c. Importance of religion:

31.5%	Most important
18.3%	2nd in importance
23.3%	3rd in importance
16.9%	4th in importance
10.0%	Least important

9d. Importance of literature:

8.5%	Most important
19.2%	2nd in importance
16.9%	3rd in importance
16.4%	4th in importance
39.0%	Least important

9e. Importance of language:

58.8%	Most important
14.0%	2nd in importance
10.0%	3rd in importance
11.8%	4th in importance
5.4%	Least important

Percentage of people responding "most important"

58.8%	Language
31.5%	Religion
17.3%	History
15.0%	Culture
8.5%	Literature

10. How much homework is assigned?

0.4%	None
8.0%	Too little
67.6%	Fair amount
16.9%	Much
7.1%	Too much

11. When I was in Greece, I found that I could:

9.2%	Understand very little
30.1%	Understand enough
51.0%	Understand a lot
41.5%	Read street signs
38.8%	Read advertisements
26.5%	Read newspapers
1.5%	Not be understood
4.6%	Be poorly understood
54.4%	Be easily understood

APPENDIX F

Questionnaire for the Studies of Greek Language and Culture
in Our Community School System in the USA   *(N=244)*

I. Personal Background

c) I was born: 43.3%   In Greece

                          56.7%   In the US or elsewhere, not Greece

My spouse was born: 54.6%   In Greece

                          45.4%   In the US or elsewhere, not Greece

Ethnic background of self and/or spouse if not Greek:

II. Evaluation

1. How would you rate the number of classroom hours per week?

                          23.3%   Inadequate

                          65.6%   Adequate

                          11.0%   More than adequate

2. How many classroom hours per week are devoted to your child's instruction in Greek?

                          4.6%   1 hour

                          21.1%   2 hours

                          14.7%   3 hours

                          26.1%   4 hours

                          15.1%   5 hours

                          11.9%   6 hours

6.4%   More than 6 hours

3.876   Mean classroom time spent on Greek

3. Rate the skills that you think should be emphasized in language instruction, in order of importance.

3a. Importance of reading:

22.9%   Most important

24.2%   2nd in importance

45.4%   3rd in importance

7.5%   Least important

3b. Importance of writing:

13.7%   Most important

16.3%   2nd in importance

18.9%   3rd in importance

51.1%   Least important

3c. Importance of speaking:

67.0%   Most important

20.4%   2nd in importance

7.0%   3rd in importance

5.7%   Least important

3d. Importance of comprehension:

36.2%   Most important

34.8%   2nd in importance

12.1%   3rd in importance

17.0%   Least important

Percentage of people responding "most important"

67.0%	Speaking
36.2%	Comprehension
22.8%	Reading
13.7%	Writing

4. *In you opinion, what should be the most important areas in your child's school curriculum?*

4a. Importance of culture:

15.4%	Most important
30.8%	2nd in importance
27.1%	3rd in importance
16.7%	4th in importance
10.0%	Least important

4b. Importance of history:

12.5%	Most important
19.6%	2nd in importance
24.1%	3rd in importance
28.6%	4th in importance
15.2%	Least important

4c. Importance of religion:

20.2%	Most important
23.3%	2nd in importance
23.3%	3rd in importance
14.3%	4th in importance
18.8%	Least important

4d. Importance of literature:

10.0%	Most important
22.2%	2nd in importance
7.2%	3rd in importance
21.3%	4th in importance
39.4%	Least important

4e. Importance of language:

83.0%	Most important
9.2%	2nd in importance
4.8%	3rd in importance
2.6%	4th in importance
0.4%	Least important

Percentage of people responding "most important"

83.0%	Language
20.2%	Religion
15.4%	Culture
12.5%	History
10.0%	Literature

5. In you opinion, how much homework is assigned?

11.5%	Too little
71.8%	A fair amount
10.6%	Much
6.2%	Too much

6. *How much Greek is spoken in your home?*

8.5%	None
27.2%	A little
34.0%	A fair amount
30.2%	A lot

7. *How often do you travel to Greece with your family?*

20.6%	Never
47.4%	Occasionally
32.0%	Frequently

8. *If you do travel to Greece, how well does your child communicate with native speakers?*

20.5%	Poorly
34.6%	Fairly well
44.9%	Quite well

9. *How involved are you and your family with a Greek community in America?*

6.9%	Not at all
30.6%	Minimally
62.5%	Quite a lot

10. *Do you subscribe to a Greek-language newspaper or magazine?*

60.4%	No
39.6%	Yes

11. *If there is a radio or TV program in the Greek language in your community, how often do you listen to it?*

        13.4%   Never

        32.8%   Infrequently

        53.9%   Frequently

12. *Does your child read Greek-language books at home?*

        46.6%   No

        53.4%   Yes

13. *Are there Greek-speaking grandparents living in your household or nearby?*

        34.7%   No

        65.3%   Yes

14. *In your opinion, what are the most important factors governing your child's successful acquisition of Greek and culture?*

   14a. *Importance of excellent schooling:*

        43.6%   Most important

        40.4%   2nd in importance

        11.5%   3rd in importance

        4.6%   4th in importance

        0.0%   Least important

14b. Importance of a supportive home environment:

55.3%	Most important
34.7%	2nd in importance
6.4%	3rd in importance
3.7%	4th in importance
0.0%	Least important

14c. Importance of travel to Greece:

16.7%	Most important
13.3%	2nd in importance
43.3%	3rd in importance
24.8%	4th in importance
1.9%	Least important

14d. Importance of living in a Greek neighborhood:

5.7%	Most important
8.3%	2nd in importance
29.2%	3rd in importance
53.6%	4th in importance
3.1%	Least important

14e. Importance of other:

42.4%	Most important
6.1%	2nd in importance
12.1%	3rd in importance
15.2%	4th in importance
24.2%	Least important

Percentage of people responding "most important"

55.3%	Supportive home environment
43.6%	Excellent schooling
42.4%	Other
16.7%	Travel to Greece
5.7%	Living in Greek neighborhood

15. *Does your child have a Greek pen pal?*

83.9%	No
16.1%	Yes

APPENDIX G

Dukakis, Michael S. (*Honorary*)
Professor of Political Science
Northeastern University
360 Huntington Avenue
202 Meserve Hall
Boston, MA 02115

Franklin, Phyllis
Executive Director
Modern Language Association of America
10 Astor Place
New York, NY 10003

Friedl, Ernestine
Professor Emerita of Cultural Anthropology
Department of Cultural Anthropology
Duke University
108 Social Science
Durham, NC 27708

Gittleman, Sol
Professor of German
Alice and Nathan Gantcher Professor of Judaic Studies
Senior Vice President and Provost
Tufts University
Medford, MA 02155-5555

Gondicas, Dimitri
Executive Director of the Program in Hellenic Studies
Lecturer in Hellenic Studies
Joseph Henry House
Princeton University
Princeton, NJ 08544

MacLean, Mary Ann S.
Member, Illinois State Board of Education
15330- Old School Road
Mettawa, IL 60048

Millstone, David
Teacher
Marion W. Cross School
P.O. Box 900, Church Street
Norwich, VT 05055

Oller, John
Professor and Head
Department of Communicative Disorders
Director of the Doris B. Hawthorne Center for Special Education
and Communicative Disorders
University of Southwestern Louisiana
200 East University
Lafayette, LA 70504-8401

Papagapitos, Vasos
Vice President
Travel Dynamics
132 East 70th Street
New York, NY 10021

Patrikalakis, Nicholas
Kawasaki Professor of Engineering
Massachusetts Institute of Technology, Room 5-428
77 Massachusetts Avenue
Cambridge, MA 02139-4307

Patrikis, Peter
Director
The Language Consortium
111 Grove Street
P.O. Box 208295
New Haven, CT 06520-8295

Sarbanes, The Honorable Paul *(Honorary)*
Senator from Maryland
309 Hart Senate Building
Washington, DC 20510

Scoccimara, Manita
Citizen-at-large
Former Member, Board of Trustees, American Farm School (Thessaloniki)
16 Laurel Lane
Greenwich, CT 06830

Scott, William
Humanities Distinguished Research Professor and Professor of Classics
Dartmouth College
Hinman Box 6086
Hanover, NH 03755

Snowe, The Honorable Olympia *(Honorary)*
Senator from Maine
250 Russell Senate Building
Washington, DC 20510

Sofronas, Demosthenes P.
Citizen-at-large
Postmaster
Norwich, VT 05055

Stefanis, Anthony
566 Arden Oak Court
Atlanta, GA 30305

Tagopoulos, Constance
Professor of Comparative Literature and Modern Greek
Coordinator of the Modern Greek Program
Department of European Languages and Literatures
Queens College (CUNY)
Flushing, New York 11367-1597

Van Buskirk, Jean
Director Emerita
Sisters Program
114 Ridgewood Road
Baltimore, MD 21210

APPENDIX H

Acknowledgments:

Thanks go to Dr. Nicholas Kladopoulos, Director of Greek Education for the Archdiocese, and to Maria Makedon, Assistant Director, for their cooperation and continuing interest.

We owe a very special expression of gratitude to Dimitra Colovos, who performed yeoman service throughout in arranging regional hearings, distributing questionnaires, translating materials, and being a most reliable and ready resource. She maintained her pleasant disposition and thoroughgoing efficiency at all times.

We also wish to thank the many hostesses who took such good care of us at each of our hearings, and the parents, teachers, students, and priests who shared so eloquently and passionately their devotion to - and fears regarding - the Greek language and culture.

Finally, we wish to thank the following consultants who participated in public hearings: Warren Cooke, Partner, Milbank, Tweed, Hadley, and McCloy (Flushing); Michael Intoccia, Director, Rassias Institute at Harold Washington College, and Leona Mirza, Teacher (Chicago); and Saul Cooper, Film producer (Los Angeles).

Source of quotations: Louis G. Kelly, 25 *Centuries of Language Teaching* (Rowley, Massachusetts: Newbury House, 1969): Augustine, p. 35; Comenius, pp. 38-39; Lemare, p. 11.

APPENDIX I

The Archdiocesan School System

The Archdiocesan School System comprises of pre-school centers, kindergartens, elementary, junior high schools, high schools and afternoon Greek language schools and classes for adults. There are 20 Greek American parochial day schools currently functioning in the United States with a total enrollment of about 4,200 students for the 1998-99 school year. Within the more than 500 Greek communities in the United States, there are 285 Greek Afternoon School programs comprised of nearly 20,000 students, from 6 to 15 years of age and taught by nearly 1,000 Greek teachers.

Directory of Greek-American Day Schools

CALIFORNIA

Holy Trinity Orthodox School
999 Brotherhood Way
San Francisco, CA 94132
Tel/Fax: (415) 584-8451
HolyTrinitySchool@worldnet.att.net
Principal: Fr. Anthony Kosturos
Vice-Principal: Lorraine Lingonis
Founded: 1971
Kindergarten to eighth grade

St. Nicholas School
9501 Balboa Boulevard
Northridge, CA 91325
Tel.: (818) 886-6751
Principal: Mrs. Janice Mattner
Founded: 1977
Pre-kindergarten to eighth grade

FLORIDA

St. John's Greek Orthodox Day School
2418 Swann Avenue
Tampa, FL 33609
Tel.: (813) 876-4569
Fax: (813) 877-4923
Principal: Mr. James J. Larkin
Founded: 1967
Pre-kindergarten to eighth grade

ILLINOIS

Koraes Greek-American School
11025-45 So. Roberts Road
Palos Hills, IL 60465
Tel.: (708) 974-3402
Fax: (708) 974-0179
Principal: Mrs. Betty Kourasis
Founded: 1910
Kindergarten to eighth grade

Plato Academy
Holy Cross Church
7560 S. Archer Road
Justice, IL 60458
Tel.: (708) 594-2040
Fax: (708) 594-8362
Principal: Dr. Catherine Antonopoulos
Founded: 1952
Pre-kindergarten to eighth grade

Socrates Greek American School
6041 W. Diversey Avenue
Chicago, IL 60639
Tel.: (773) 622-5979
Principal: Mr. William D. Smith
Founded: 1907
Pre-school to eighth grade

MARYLAND

Hellenic American Academy
10701 South Glen Road
Potomac, MD 20854
Tel.: (301) 299-1566
Principal: Mrs. Elaine Lailas
Founded: 1988
Pre-K to fifth grade

MASSACHUSETTS

Hellenic American School of Holy Trinity
41 Broadway
Lowell, MA 01854
Tel.: (978) 453-5422
Fax: (978) 970-0935
Principal: Dr. James Demos
Founded: 1909
Kindergarten to sixth grade

NEW YORK

Cathedral School
319 East 74th Street
New York, NY 10021
Tel.: (212) 249-2840
Fax: (212) 249-2847
Principal: Mr. Minos Kazepis
Founded: 1949
Nursery to eighth grade

"C. Goulandris-T. Tsolainos"
Greek Orthodox Parochial School of St. Spyridon
120 Wadsworth Avenue
New-York, NY 10033
Tel.: (212) 795-6870
Fax: (212) 795-4758
Principal: Dr. Andreas Zachariou
Founded: 1959
Pre-Kindergarten to eighth grade

Greek-American Institute
3573 Bruckner Boulevard
Bronx, NY 10461
Tel.: (718) 823-2393
Fax: (718) 823-0790
Principal: Mrs. Angela Kusulas
Founded: 1912
Pre-Kindergarten to eighth grade

A. Fantis Parochial School
195 State Street
Brooklyn, NY 11201
Tel.: (718) 624-0501
Fax: (718) 246-5711
Principal: Mrs. Aphrodite Galitsis
Founded: 1963
Pre-kindergarten to ninth grade

Soterios Ellenas Parochial School
224 18th Street
Brooklyn, NY 11215
Tel.: (718) 499-5900
Fax: (718) 832-3712
Principal: Dr. George Melikokis
Founded: 1966
Nursery to eighth grade

Three Hierarchs Parochial School
1724 Avenue P
Brooklyn, NY 11229
Tel.: (718) 375-1885
Fax: (718) 375-0006
Principal: Mr. James Yeannakopoulos
Founded: 1975
Nursery to eighth grade

**D. and G. Kaloidis Parochial School of Holy Cross
Greek Orthodox Church**
8502 Ridge Boulevard
Brooklyn, NY 11209
Tel.: (718) 836-8096
Fax: (718) 836-4772
Principal: Dr. Bernadette L. McNulty
Nursery to eighth grade

St. Demetrios Greek-American School of Astoria
30-03 30th Drive
Astoria, NY 11102
Tel.: (718) 728-1754
Fax: (718) 726-3482
Supervising Principal: Mr. Constantine Rizopoulos

High School (Grades 7-12)
Founded: 1975

Middle School (Grades 4-6)
30-03 30th Drive
Astoria, NY 11102
Tel.: (718) 726-6734
Founded: 1957

St. Demetrios Annex
(Pre-K to 3)
22-30 33rd St
Astoria, NY 11105
Tel. (718) 728-1100
Founded: 1957

**Jamaica Day School of St. Demetrios and
Archbishop Iakovos High School**
84-35 152nd Street
Jamaica, NY 11432
Tel.: (718) 526-2622
Fax: (718) 526-1680
Principal: Mr. Costas Loukeris
Pre-K to eighth grade
Founded: 1967

High School (Grades 9-12)
Founded: 1980

School of the Metamorphosis (Transfiguration)
98-07 38th Avenue
Corona, NY 11368
Tel.: (718) 478-8181
Fax: (718) 478-8199
Principal: Mrs. Helen Lydakis
Founded: 1967
Pre-K to ninth grade

William Spyropoulos Greek-American Day School of St. Nicholas
43-15 196th Street
Flushing, NY 11358
Tel.: (718) 357-5583
Fax: (718) 357-5475
Principal: Mrs. Chris Arlis
Founded: 1977
Nursery to eighth grade

TEXAS

Annunciation Orthodox School
3600 Yoakum Boulevard
Houston, TX 77006
Tel.: (713) 620-3600
Fax: (713) 620-3605
Principal: Mr. Mark Kelly
Founded: 1970
Pre-school to eighth grade